CHRISTMAS SHORT-CUTS

by

Adeline Rosemire

Meridian
PUBLISHING, INC.

San Jose, California

Meridian
PUBLISHING, INC.

San Jose, California

Published by Meridian Publishing, Inc.

ISBN 0-9640044-1-0

Printed and bound in the United States of America.

Contents

Introduction

Index

Introduction

You'll notice that some of the chapters in *Christmas Shortcuts* are very brief: some are only one or two pages in length. As you know, it seems as though no one has any time to read about, let alone *enjoy,* the holidays. If you had the time to read long missives and intricate cookbooks during the holiday season, you wouldn't be reading this book now, would you?

Christmas Shortcuts was written to help you eliminate the hassle and hurry that many people associate with the holiday season. If the season makes you break into a cold sweat, hives, or worse, this book will help you put all that behind you and provide you with a way to truly *enjoy* the holidays.

Remember, the best traditions provide what everyone wants throughout the year: love, acceptance, and the feeling that they're contributing.

For those of you who *need* these shortcuts (and you know who you are...), buckle up!

Special note to readers:
During the holidays, *everything* will take longer than planned. This is just one of the accepted holiday tenants: everything is working against you. From snowstorms and power outages, to long lines and snarled traffic, you're going up against natural forces. You can make the holidays more enjoyable this year, and for years to come, with just a sprinkle of forethought.

Phone numbers, addresses and web addresses were current at the time of publication. This booklet will be updated next year with new gift ideas, phone numbers, addresses and web addresses.

Chapter 1

It only takes three basic steps to ease your holiday pressures, but they're crucial.

Step 1: Make a gift list.

Writing your gift list on paper is half the battle. Include your spouse, significant others, family members, friends, co-workers, employees, service people, nannies, teachers, gardener, pets, friends' pets, maid and butler (I should be so lucky...)

You can and should use this list *throughout the year* (or at least during the last few minutes of your Christmas shopping frenzy...)

Once your list is compiled, the math-inclined among you may divide the 'gift budget' amount by the number of gifts, to determine the average cost of your gifts. Budget? Did someone say 'budget'? Well, it will give you a chance to set a reasonable amount to spend. (This will *theoretically* help you keep the balance of your credit card accounts below the stratospheric level.)

The exercise of committing your gift list to paper is actually liberating, since it gives you a framework in which to function. It's also efficient, since the names on your gift list won't vary much from year to year (this is a perfect use for a computer). In fact, glancing back at gift lists from previous years will help you vary selections, note trends, avoid duplication, and update everyone's gift preferences and sizes.

To end the obligation of 'duty' gifts, send early holiday cards to everyone on your gift list explaining your new stance and plans to prune your gift list during this season of excess. Send these early-warning cards to: former neighbors, relatives you don't like, or co-workers you're reluctant to offend. They'll probably be relieved, *provided* that you give them ample warning.

Optional: Create a list of gifts you would like to receive, just in case someone asks for it!

Step 2: Take 10 minutes and list everything you would like to accomplish during the holidays.

Read your list and select the three or four choices that are most important to you. Do something truly courageous by deleting low-priority items.

Remember: Making a list helps you define, and accomplish, your goals.

Step 3: Purchase a manila folder.

Label the folder 'Holidays' or whatever you wish. As time goes by, fill the folder with lists, community event calendars, holiday 'idea' articles from newspapers and magazines, and other holiday information that you find of interest.

Turning clutter into an organized system increases your efficiency and reduces your stress. Who couldn't use a little of that during the holidays?

Take control. Don't let the holidays become a reactive catastrophe instead of a planned event.

Timing: Give yourself plenty of time to get things done. Being rushed is the biggest cause of holiday stress. Outline a loose plan and start your holiday preparations early.

Optional: Start a Christmas Club account at your bank; it's a painless way to avoid huge bills at the end of the holiday season.

Chapter 2

Advanced holiday shortcuts (also known as 'using folders')

First step: Purchase 3 or 4 manila file folders.

Second step: Label the folders as follows:
a. Holiday Decorations
b. Holiday Events
c. Holiday Gift List
   (start a folder this year and keep it for future reference)
d. Holiday Food (optional)

Third step:
Add materials that are pertinent to each folder throughout the year or during the holiday season. Pertinent materials might include: magazine and newspaper clippings, recipes, community 'holiday calendar of events', and catalogs (with pages of interest marked and recipients' names noted).

Optional: The following strategy is for families with busy schedules (or anyone with a partner whose emotions run high).

Purchase a large activity calendar and attach it (along with a pencil and connecting string) to the refrigerator door, or next to the phone that your family uses the most. Have everyone write in their individual holiday schedules (include school plays, company events, dental appointments, parties and special visits). This is where you can also add and *delegate* holiday tasks!

Chapter 3

The beauty and ease of using catalogs

Shopping from catalogs is probably the most peaceful method of
holiday shopping. You'll benefit by eliminating 'mall crawl' time,
sparing your resources and energy, bypassing long lines, and
avoiding a gift-wrapping marathon (unless you enjoy
that kind of thing!)

Catalog capabilities/strategy:

• Order all or most of your gift selections (food, clothing, games, music,
  entertainment, electronic gadgets, gifts for pets, etc.) from catalogs to avoid
  long cashier lines
• Have your selections gift-wrapped and sent to you from the catalogs
• Have your selections gift-wrapped and sent directly to the recipient
  (great idea if you're flying or taking a long drive to your holiday destination)
• Order food for your holiday dinner from catalogs, and avoid the stress and
  pressure of preparing the 'perfect' holiday meal
• Order a gift certificate from a catalog which suits the gift recipient's tastes.
  Package the catalog and gift certificate in a large envelope to present at the
  holidays, or wrap both in a box

Catalog tips:

• Begin to save suitable catalogs in September or earlier. The holiday deluge
  usually starts in August. When you see a potential gift in a catalog, either
  fold the corner of the page and write the recipient's name next to the item,
  or use a self-sticking note to mark the spot.
• Collect catalogs and gift ideas for several months. You'll need a 'cooling
  down' period to be able to select gifts rationally, as well as do some
  comparison shopping.
• If you purchase holiday presents early and need to keep them from prying
  eyes, simply put the gifts in one of your empty suitcases.

- Read about the return policy before you place an order from a catalog. Some companies make returning an item very easy; others don't. If you're not comfortable with a catalog's return policy, don't place an order.
- Remember to note purchases on your gift list.
- Keep all purchase receipts in one envelope until after the holidays, in case someone needs to return or exchange a gift.
- After the holidays, shop the catalogs for holiday sales items to use next year.

Rationale:

You can't beat the convenience of catalog shopping. Plus, the gifts are guaranteed to come in their own shipping boxes, which can be used as gift boxes!

Special note:

Please refer to the 'List of Catalogs' chapter for catalog addresses, toll-free numbers, and Internet addresses.

Chapter 4
Gift list preparation and tips

(also known as 'keeping a cool head')

With the commercialism of the holidays, it's sometimes difficult to remember that the holiday season does not entirely revolve around gifts. (I know, I know; try telling that to a 4-year-old.) In fact, the number one complaint about Christmas is that gift-giving has gotten out of hand. Don't fall into the holiday trap set by stores and advertisers trying to make our holiday celebrations as elaborate and *expensive* as possible.

Strategy
Try to put yourself into the mindframe of the gift recipient. The key is to think about *what they'd like to receive*— not what you want to give them. You've reached the pinnacle of gift-giving when perspectives and ideas converge into one gift; it's guaranteed to make the gift exchange fun for the giver and givee.

Don't forget to make notes of which gifts were received especially well this year. Also note people's wishes. This is something you can do during the rest of the year, too. Start now!

Kids as consumers
Ask children "What are you *giving* for Christmas", rather than "What are you *getting?*" You may want to teach compassion to kids by including a new toy or item in your gift list for a less fortunate child or family. Many communities and organizations have 'gift drop-off' programs; just call your city's main phone number for more information. For a true sense of Christmas, request permission to personally deliver the gifts to a needy family. You may also contact the Toys for Tots office or the Salvation Army in your area.

How to make your gift list shorter
•Ask friends if they'd mind skipping the gift-giving ritual this year; consider substituting a lunch date instead.
•Prune, or at least limit, your gift list. This year, just tell your friend, neighbor or co-worker that you'd prefer not to exchange gifts. It's very likely that your friends are trying to pare down their gift lists, too.

- Draw names so that each person buys a gift for one individual instead of everyone.
- Cut down on the number of gifts you buy. Try giving 'family gifts' at the holidays— one gift for the entire household instead of individual gifts for everyone. Save the individual presents for birthdays.
- Give gifts to children only.
- Set an age limit for gifts to children.
- Don't give gifts to peoples' pets.

It's all in the timing

Think of a gift category or theme to fit everyone: movies, gift certificates, electronic gadgets, magazine subscriptions, a computer game for the entire family. Even more time-efficient, choose gifts that don't require shopping— magazine subscriptions, museum memberships, movie gift certificates, theater tickets, or contributions in a recipient's name to their favorite non-profit organization.

Special note: Place early gift orders for holiday plants and flowers. To have floral gifts sent from a recipient's local florist, call 1- (their area code)-555-1212, and ask for the (substitute city or town's name) florist. Example: San Francisco Florist (415) 555-1212. After reaching a florist, just describe what type plant or flowers you would like to send and pay for it using your credit card.

And one for all...

- One way to decrease your shopping effort is to buy everyone the same gift. You'll save time (picture those crowded stores/malls) and money by buying in quantity.
- Don't waste time shopping for the perfect gift for someone who's hard to please; instead, honor them with a gift certificate.

Geographical considerations

- Buy gift certificates from stores that are located near the recipient's home.
- Ask the gift recipients for a list of their favorite local stores.

Shopping Tips— the physical element

- Dress comfortably and carry a backpack to leave your hands free.
- Streamline your purse and pockets. Carry only the essential credit cards, identification, gift list, checkbook, pen or pencil. Your feet will thank you.
- Preplan your trip by listing the stores you wish to visit, mapping an orderly shopping route, and numbering the stores accordingly.
- Take your address book with you when you shop, so you can have packages mailed directly to the recipients from the store.
- Get a box with every item you purchase— the extra boxes will come in handy during Operation Gift-Wrap.

Receipts

Keep all receipts in a separate envelope. Note the gift item and recipient's name. If you shop early in the season and then discover later that the purchased item has been discounted, take it back to the store. As long as you have the receipt, chances are they'll refund the difference.

Gifts of time and skill

Make a coupon for any service you can offer:

- cooking lessons
- baby-sitting
- an afternoon of organizing a closet or kitchen
- a trip to a museum, etc., or an event of the recipient's choice
- reading or storytelling
- a computer lesson or software installation
- a semester's worth of weekly tutoring
- neck, back or foot massages
- a lunch, dinner, movie, or an errand day for someone who doesn't drive a vehicle
- a lunch with your mom (or dad). Be sure to specify a certain month to increase the degree of your committment.
- fix-it services (especially for older adults)
- a hour of weeding, raking or mowing
- a season's worth of snow blowing or snow shoveling, or a spring and/or fall window-washing session

Gifts for 'hard-to-shop-for' people or those who have 'everything' (This includes Mom who has mutated into the Woman-Who-Has-Everything-and-Wants-Nothing.)

- a picture frame
- 'gourmet' fruit or candy
- an invitation to a special restaurant (with or without you)
- restaurant gift certificates
- a contribution to their favorite cause or charity
- generic gift certificates from shopping malls (for use in a local mall's shops)
- a department store gift certificate (attach with ribbon to an ornament)
- a magazine subscription

Types of gifts and/or catalog categories

- clothing
- entertainment
- food
- functional gifts
- gift certificates
- jewelry
- music
- perfume— consider matching perfume to a CD of a similar name, etc.
- recreational gifts
- recyclable gifts
- romantic gifts
- toys/games for children, adults or family

With that said, let's plunge into the list of gift ideas with gusto!

Chapter 5
Great gift ideas for infants through young adults

Newborns
- soft toys
- diaper service
- stocks, bonds and/or mutual funds for a college education
- a trustee savings account at a bank (you'll need the newborn's Social Security Number)
- a personalized Christmas tree ornament (with their name and the year in which it was given)
- a crystal baby bottle (comes with a silver plated tarnish-resistant cup, for the baby who has everything)

Toddlers
- stocks, bonds and/or mutual funds for their college education
- coloring books and crayons, picture books
- toys marked 'ages 3 and under', including stuffed bears
- Disney videos

Books for tots
Christmas with Teddy Bear (Dial Books for Young Readers; $12.99), by Jacqueline McQuade, will thrill tots as they hear about young Teddy eagerly counting down the days until Christmas

Young children
- stocks, bonds and/or mutual funds for their financial and college education (include a $5 or $10 bill for them to spend or save in the very near future)
- silver dollars wrapped in a small scarf, muffler or silver wrapping
- animal slippers
- FunSeeker Binoculars (Bnox; $12.99), prefocused with panoramic or telephoto-lens style, perfect for discovering nature
- a cut-glass prism
- the boardgame 'Moneywise Kids' (Aristoplay; $15), an easy, enjoyable way for children to learn about money while improving their math skills
- a package of paper with markers, tape, stick-ons, etc.

- a rubber stamp with the child's name
- a small plant
- a gift certificate to a pet store for supplies (or a pet). *Warning:This could be the loose cannon of gifts; either be prepared for anything or don't risk giving this gift at all.*

Special note:
Remember to send a card, letter or item in the mail to youngsters, they love getting their own mail.

Gifts for grandparents to give to their grandchildren

- a 'memory' concrete stepping stone kit for the garden (from Solutions catalog), in which to preserve small handprints, artwork, etc.
- an advent calendar (a nice item to mail)
- a small overnight bag, including a small bar of soap, a miniature tube of toothpaste, and face towel
- a puzzle

Note: Call the Duracell Toy Hot Line at 1-800- BEST TOYS (1-800-237-8869) to hear a pre-recorded message that lists the names and manufacturers of the current ten top toys. The list was selected by 650 kids at YMCA after-school centers, out of 24 new toys selected by toy consultants. (And you thought *you* had a great job!)

Books for young readers (ages 4-12)

- *Ben's Christmas Tale* (Dutton Children's Books; $15.99), by Toby Forward, is based upon Charles Dickens' *A Christmas Carol.* Ben is a Scroogelike mouse.
- *Pippi Longstocking's After-Christmas Party* (Viking; $13.99), by Astrid Lindgren, is available for the first time in English. Originally written in Sweden in the 1950s, readers will enjoy reading (and learning) about Swedish holiday traditions.
- *Nancy Drew*, by Carolyn Keene, and *The Hardy Boys Series*, by Franklin Dixon. These are terrific gifts for pre-teen readers and are available in the original, classic or updated versions.

Pre-teens (ages 8-12)

- sports equipment
- battery-operated electronic games
- a hair dryer, curling iron

18

- a bicycle
- roller blades and/or accessories
- CD gift certificates

Holiday books (for children of all ages)

- *Blintzes for Blitzen* (Mixed Blessing; $8.95), by Elise and Philip Oakrend, a unique fable blending Christmas and Hanukkah traditions.
- *Kwanzaa Fun* (Kingfisher; $5.95), by Linda Robertson, helps children learn and celebrate the seven principles of Kwanzaa, a tradition celebrated in many African-American communities.
- *'Twas the night before Christmas*, by Clement Moore

Gifts for children/teenagers

- tennis, skiing, or skating lessons
- movie passes to a neighborhood theater
- a spending spree kit (cash and gift certificate to a restaurant)
- 'scrunchies' (can't have too many of these hair accessories!)
- gift certificates to fast food restaurants
- mini-hoop earrings

Gifts for teenagers/college students/twentysomethings

- membership to a discount warehouse, health spa or gym
- cookbooks from the 'healthy eating' category, or a super-simple cookbook
- health and/or car insurance for 6 months
- AAA emergency car service
- a gasoline credit card for 6 months (you might want to indicate a monthly limit)
- a sound system for the car
- a gift certificate to a car wash
- a leather scheduler/calendar
- 'Walkman' type headphones
- a digital bedside clock
- an answering machine, call waiting service, or a cellular phone
- a pager and monthly service
- a small microwave oven, small refrigerator, or expresso machine
- a commuter mug

- stationery, postal stamps, writing pads, markers, folders, or a complete desk supply kit (include a paperback dictionary, if desired)
- food gifts that need no refrigeration (use bags of popped popcorn as filler, so that even the packing will be edible)
- mini backpacks
- a journal
- a stun gun or pepper spray
- lifestyle furnishings or decor for their dorm room or apartment (See 'List of Catalogs' chapter.)
- specific gifts that may be needed in their 'new life'

Gift certificates or event passes for teenagers/college students/twentysomethings
(and people who just think young)

Teenagers are the consummate consumers and readily accept gift certificates or passes.
- *Gift certificates for music, entertainment, education or luxuries*
- CDs (compact discs)
- movie/theater tickets (for out-of-state recipients, check their local chain theater)
- passes to a neighborhood cinema or theater chain in their area (hide the tickets in a bag of popcorn or in a rolled up movie poster)
- video rental gift certificates
- prepaid phone cards from 'Future Call' (1-800-333-8735)
- a coupon for on-line computer services
- a gift certificate to an office supply house or computer store
- gas station credit card (especially for young drivers)
- car wash gift certificates
- a gift certificate to a florist
- a gift certificate to a manicure specialist
- exercise classes
- a rejuvenating weekend at a health spa
- gift certificates to a nearby coffee house (Present the gift certificate in a wacky or artsy mug. Wrap with cellophane and tie with ribbon. These certificates provide a great excuse for the recipient to ask someone to accompany them. "My aunt sent this gift certificate to me and I wondered if you'd join me?"

Gift certificates for food from:
- local caterers that serve and deliver to individual college students
- a pizzeria or restaurant
- a 'natural foods' store
- a bakery
- an ice cream parlor

Gift certificates for clothing and other items from:
- a department store
- a favorite clothing store or upscale clothing store
- a discount store (Target, etc.)
- a sporting goods store
- a catalog

Create 'gift kits' that relate to a young individual's interests or hobbies

- a car-care kit: items from an auto supply shop or catalog (bucket, hose and nozzle, cleansers, waxes, sponges, lint-free cloths)
- a party kit: various supplies available at party supply stores, stationery and drug stores
- a writer's kit: writing tablets or paper, pens and erasers
- a social butterfly kit: include concert gift certificates or guidebooks to a museum, or a map and 'walking tour' directions (plus gift certificates for refreshments along the way.) Walking tour packages are available in some cities; contact the visitor's center in the desired city.
- a spending-spree kit: wrap cash in a box and label it 'Spending Spree!' (You might want to combine it with a gift certificate from their favorite mall restaurant.)
- a joke kit (have friends or relatives of the recipient record new or favorite jokes, or special notes)

New product alert! CD calendars (with sensational artwork and photos) are great for those people lucky enough to have computers.

Chapter 6
Gift kits
Generic Kits— put these together yourself!

* car-care kit (from an auto supply shop or catalogs): bucket, hose nozzle, cleansers, waxes, sponges, lint-free cloths
* baking or chef kit: include holiday-themed pot holders and towels (use the towel as wrapping material) and kitchen gadgets such as an apple corer, garlic press, steamer, cheese grater, mushroom slicer and brush
* gardener's kit: items or gift certificates from a catalog, garden center or hardware store. Tie a gift certificate to a live plant or flowers.
* photographer's kit: color and black-and-white film, lens cleaner, gift certificate for photo development, photo album
* reunion/travel kit: ideal for a buddy that you haven't seen in a while— send a plane ticket to meet you halfway for a reunion
* comfort kit: gift certificate to a bath and body products store or catalog; tie the gift certificate to a luxurious item
* walker's kit: soothing foot lotion, comfortable walking shoes, top-quality socks (or a gift certificate for foot-related items)

Gift kits that appeal to the recipient's interests or hobbies.

* an artist's kit: a gift certificate to an art store, art catalog and/or museum
* a couch potato kit: universal remote control, bean bag chair, pillows, blankets, popcorn, comforter, food tray, movies on tape, beverage holder to keep liquids cold or hot
* a lady-of-leisure basket: many cosmetic departments of stores will custom design a holiday gift basket with the fragrance and accessory items of your choice; select from an assortment of pre-arranged holiday baskets, or create your own basket
* a hair maintenance kit (especially popular with teenagers): shampoos, conditioners, hair brush, dryer, superdrying towels (found at your local beauty supply store), a gift coupon for a hair styling — just put it all in a basket and tie with a bow
* a new mom kit: soft music, magazines, aspirin, warm and snugly clothes
* a newlyweds kit: chocolates, champagne, bed and breakfast pre-paid weekend stay, restaurant gift certificates

- a newly-divorced kit: can easily be made up using items from catalogs, malls and stores (don't forget to add a humorous item to take the pressure off their situation)
- a parents' kit: catalog gift certificates, or a personalized coupon for a lunch or dinner out with you (specify a certain month of the year to help you follow through)
- a pet-oriented kit for people: gift certificates to pet stores for supplies (or a pet)
- a holiday memory kit: create a kit from a camera or nearby drug store, include a camera (35mm, pocket size, single-use, or Polaroid), prepaid development mailers, frames, albums, film, etc.
- a diner's kit: a gift certificate to a restaurant, along with the restaurant's menu, and perhaps movie tickets
- a swimmer's kit: beach towel, goggles, swim suit, swimming lessons, beach bag, sunscreen, trashy novel

 ## Gift kits for newlyweds

- a cookbook, or a personalized cookbook of your own filled with family recipes
- heavy-duty can or bottle openers
- knives and/or cutting boards
- appliances, such as a blender, crockpot, toaster, juicer, microwave oven, expresso maker or coffee machine
- linens, blankets, comforters
- a honeymoon kit (include chocolate and champagne)
- a little toolbox filled with nails, picture hooks, a hammer, and a screw driver

Chapter 7
Gifts for specific lifestyles and careers

Gifts for enthusiasts or lifestyles

- aviators (See 'List of Catalogs' chapter.)
- caregivers (See 'List of Catalogs' chapter, the 'Health and Lifestyle' section.)
- gamblers: books about gambling, lottery tickets, a weekend stay at a gambling resort
- Bingo players: Bingo stampers, carry-all bags, Bingo card stands (Note: Bingo promotes physical activity and socializing)
- nature lovers: equipment for hiking or biking, bird feeders, binoculars
- readers: a book and video of a classic movie, a brass bookmark (See Levengers in the 'List of Catalogs' chapter.)
- sports fans (including fishermen, as well as football fans, etc.): gift certificates to sports catalogs, sports apparel (with their favorite team's logo), tickets to sporting events, magazine subscriptions for their favorite sport, autographed equipment, collector cards, video tapes, books, sports-related computer software
- travelers: a gift certificate or item from a travel catalog; a compact pillow, alarm or umbrella designed for travel; a waist-strap money holder; luggage tags; eye shades; a seven-day pill case; a panoramic or underwater disposable camera; a compass; a travel guide or language dictionary; or a prepaid trip with or without you!

(See also the 'Gift Kits' chapter.)

Gifts for the career-minded

- generic 'career' gifts: gift certificate to a catalog or store specializing in specific pursuits
- engineers: gift certificates to a local computer, book or hardware store; stress-busting toys; magazine subscription
- lawyers: paperweights, letter openers, humorous or stress-busting items
- medical professionals: stress relief items, hand exercisers, a day at a sauna, the new colorful stethoscopes, coffee mug, fruit-of-the-month gift
- teachers: homemade edibles, rubber stamps, stickers, note pads, scarves, gift certificate to Oriental Trading catalog (See 'List of Catalogs' chapter), bookstore or children's store gift certificate, and/or holiday ornaments. Caution: don't fall prey to 'apple motif overkill'.

Career/business-related gifts

• *job hunters*: gift certificate for on-line services or an Internet service provider; gift certificate to an office supply store for resume paper and envelopes; tuition assistance for career-related classes; an answering machine or gift certificate for a voice-messaging service from the phone company; humor books or tapes to soothe tired spirits after a long day of job hunting; tickets to a show and/or a good restaurant

• *clients or boss:* gift certificate to a beauty or health spa, flowers, gourmet basket, engraved paperweight or mug, jogging suit, a sweatshirt with his or her favorite team's logo

• *fellow employees*: rather than giving small individual presents, why not pool your money and purchase an item that everyone can enjoy such as a radio, small television, microwave oven, expresso maker, etc?

Personalized gifts for everyone

• *personal business-size cards*
Have these produced at a quick-copy center; include the person's name, address, phone number (optional), as well as their on-line address, if desired. The cards are very convenient to hand to new/old friends, at social functions, or to include in a greeting card or letter. You're always free to add a clever or humorous title such as household engineer, artist and comedian, family CEO, teacher, student, technical monarch, etc. Cards are also convenient to hand to personal shoppers, service and repair people.

• *stationery*
This is available from catalogs and stationery stores (including personal-ized note cards, memo cubes, cards, etc.)

Chapter 8
Gifts based on interests or hobbies

Nature

Adopt a redwood tree or an elephant in someone's name (see list below). You can make a contribution in the name of your gift recipient. Ask that the certificate be sent to you, as well as a letter explaining what benefitted from the recipient's help. To ensure on-time arrival, send your donation by early December. You might combine the donation with endangered-species jewelry (tiny replicas of whales, cheetahs, wolves) or key chains for the humanitarian who cares about all life.

Ocean creatures

Whales started the trend. You may adopt an orca ($35) through The Whale Museum, (206) 378-4710; a gray whale ($50) through the Tarlton Foundation, (415) 433-3163; or a humpback ($25) through the Pacific Whale Foundation, 1-800-942-5311. Adopt a dolphin ($35) through the Oceanic Society, (415) 441-1106.

Mammals and other animals

Adopt a wolf ($20) through Wolf Haven International, 1-800-448-9653. Almost all zoos have adopt-an-animal programs, from a spider ($1) to an elephant ($1,500). Call a zoo located near the gift recipient for more information.

Trees

Adopt a redwood tree ($200) or have one planted ($50) through Save-the-Redwoods League, (415) 362-2352. Adopt a acre of South American rain forest for $30 through The Nature Conservancy, 1-800-628-6860; or for $25 through The Rainforest Action Network, (415) 398-4404. Or adopt an American ancient forest grove ($50) through the Audubon Society, (916) 481-5332 or (206) 786-8020.

Magazine subscriptions (for all ages and interests)

Use magazine brokers to receive some of the least expensive magazine subscription rates available. Order subscriptions for those hard-to-shop-for people on your list. Magazines are gifts that recipients can enjoy the entire year. (To make next year's shopping even easier, magazine publishers will send you an early renewal reminder, and an easy way to renew the subscription, if you so desire.) Magazine examples: *TV Guide, Newsweek, Health, Arizona Highways, Prevention*, sports magazines, car magazines, etc. Magazine subscription brokers include: Below Wholesale Magazines, 1-800-800-0062.

Museum gifts or memberships

* a museum catalog and gift certificate
* gift certificate to a local museum's gift store (great for kids, too!)
    (See 'List of Catalogs' chapter, Museums section.)

Tickets to events, concerts, sports arenas

* Purchase tickets to a cultural performance, concert or sporting event for family members or friends. Order the tickets all at once with one phone call; in later months, everyone can meet and enjoy the event together.

Chapter 9
Inexpensive, generic, and host/hostess gifts

Gifts for families, groups, or general 'house gifts'
- self-inking address stamp or return address labels
- houseplants
- photo albums
- bird feeder and bird book
- wind chimes
- holiday potholders
- relaxation or nature tapes
- lap desk
- food gifts
- music gifts

Inexpensive gift ideas for hostesses, friends, or neighbors, etc.
These are token gifts small enough that the recipient does not feel obligated to reciprocate.
- a beautifully wrapped box of long fireplace matches (for the recipient's fireplace or barbecue)
- a note holder (Altitude is of utmost importance in order for that important message, list or photo to *rise above* the clutter. Sources: restaurant supply stores or catalogs)
- note cube (to keep by the phone)
- a small, live plant tied with a plaid ribbon, or decorated with a small ornament
- a list of city service phone numbers and the numbers of your favorite repair people to share with neighbors who have just moved in. As a special touch, include it with a small address book or journal.
- a batch of your favorite home-baked cookies. Wrap them in clear cellophane (available at florist supply or crafts stores), twist the top of the cellophane and tie with a holiday ribbon.

Unique gifts for family members

Give coupons for special favors, such as car washing or lawn mowing.

- a gift certificate for a week's worth of morning coffee at a favorite coffee bar. (Present the certificate in a commuter mug.)
- copies of old family photographs (complete with suitable frame, if desired)
- a certificate bearing the history of a family name. Present the certificates as presents, framed if desired. One company that provides this service is The Historical Research Center. The cost varies from $20 to $60. For more information, call (954) 421-0119.
- a family cookbook. Call relatives to submit favorite recipes for publishing. Print several copies to present as gifts to family members. Title the publication 'Aunt Jane's Holiday Favorites', 'Mom's Famous Recipes' or 'The Smith Family Cookbook'.
- a collection of family stories. Ask family members (from all generations) to write down and submit their favorite family stories to you. Print them up into a little booklet for each family group. Save one copy in a family history album for future generations to enjoy.

In-bulk (or one-stop-shopping) gifts for friends or relatives

- holiday-wrapped cans of gourmet pecans or other delicacies (in gift groups of twelve or more, etc.) that can be presented individually
- dining coupons
- gift certificates to major department stores

Chapter 10

Gifts for women, men and parents

Women (listed by age range)

- Women under 35 usually enjoy entertainment-oriented gifts such as video-rental coupons, record-store gift certificates, movie passes, restaurant gift certificates, or a personal color analysis (this service is available at most beauty salons)
- Women between 35 and 50 enjoy picture frames, coffee mugs, silk plants, artistically painted ceramic tile, and exercise videos
- Women over 50, in general, like food baskets filled with tea, chocolate, fruit or homemade treats

Gifts for mothers:

- Photo album; housecleaning service; a day at a spa; coupon for a haircut and styling; eye pillow; bed caddy; cloth or canvas shopping bag; kitchen gadgets; gift certificate to an adult education class (check with their local community college or adult education center), plus class materials; member ship to a health club

Men (listed by age range)

- Men under 35 usually enjoy movie passes, music store gift certificates, videos, etc.
- Men between 35-50 appreciate gift certificates to a sports equipment or hardware store
- Men over 50 typically like tickets to sports or cultural events (plus accompaniment?)

Gifts for fathers:

Books on tape that offer tips on golf, fishing, or other activities; season tickets to his favorite sport; magazine subscriptions; pocketknife; mini car vacuum; garden hose; nozzle; jogging shoes; flannel shirts; a gift certificate for hand-made custom-fitted shoes; shoe-polishing kit; garage door opener; gift certificate for an adult education class to encourage more social interaction or new interests (check with local community college or adult education center), plus class materials; membership to a health club; or a gift certificate to the Brookstone or Sharper Image catalogs (See 'List of Catalogs' chapter.)

Chapter 11

Gifts for older adults/grandparents
Personal, family-oriented items

- framed photos of the grandchildren or family, a personalized photo calendar (made at quick-copy centers), or a tee-shirt or coffee mug with family photo
- a photo album with a selection of family photos
- audio or video tapes of family gatherings (make sure they have suitable playback equipment, or present a VCR or tape player as a holiday gift!)
- audiotape or video tape of older family members as they recall the 'good old days'; make copies for family history collectors
- framed artwork by their grandchildren and/or great grandchildren

Entertainment/communications

- tapes of favorite 'classic' movies or old television programs from the '50s
- books on tape (purchase, or read and record books or short stories yourself for a personal and unique gift to be treasured)
- books with large print
- an easy-grip letter opener, personalized note paper and return address labels
- an answering machine, a cordless phone, a special telephone for the hearing or sight impaired (or phone with enlarged number display)
- a touch tone telephone with large numbers and/or memory
- a gift certificate for long-distance calls
- a tape recorder, player, earphones
- a radio or cassette player
- a personal TV with remote control
- a videocassette recorder (VCR) and installation
- a year of cable television service (if available in their area)
- a subscription to a weather channel or cable TV
- an inexpensive computer to 'get wired to the world'. These are great for keeping in touch on-line with school-age relatives or grandchildren. There are also specific services for older adults; make sure that on-line services are available in the recipient's locale.

Comfort and convenience items

- a small afghan or lap robe
- garage door opener (plus installation)
- personal coupons for pet-sitting, visits, yard work, car washing, writing letters, etc.
- an orthopedic pillow, a bed caddy, knitted slippers
- night lights or a night lamp
- a seasonal wreath
- a gift certificate for special household chores
- binoculars
- a high-quality magnifying glass or large-sheet magnifier
- under-bed storage units
- satin-covered clothes hangers
- playing cards with large faces and numbers
- a clock with large numbers
- walking shoes
- a pill cutter
- clothes or gadgets for special handicaps
- a gift certificate for a manicure and pedicure at a favorite salon
- a parakeet (with cage, food and toys)

Food gifts

- grocery store gift certificates
- food gifts (use catalogs to make your selections, of course!)
- gift boxes of meat or gourmet foods for the freezer (See 'List of Catalogs' chapter.)
- a coffee mug with tea or hot-chocolate packets
- dried or fresh fruit from Harriet and David or the Fruit-of-the-Month Club

Events/trips/transportation

- a gift certificate for car care, gas and/or a car wash
- gift certificates for cab rides; especially appropriate for an older person who no longer drives
- concert or play tickets and transportation to the event
- transportation to visit nearby friends
- tickets to a performance or concert (with you as company!) Especially good for those people who 'have everything'.
- a weekend get-away with the family to a scenic destination
- travel agency gift certificates
- a cruise (a group can purchase tickets to make the gift more affordable). Companies to consider: Carnival Cruise, 1-800-327-9501; Norwegian Cruise Line, 1-800-327-7030; and Princess Cruise, 1-800-421-0522.
- a gift certificate to an adult education class, plus class materials. This encourages social interaction and builds new interests (check with their local community college or adult education center.) After the class, buy materials for grandparents to teach their grandchildren for a mutually enjoyable, shared experience.

Gardeners

- gardening tools or equipment
- a gardening seat with wheels
- plants, seeds and/or bulbs
- a gift certificate to a garden center

Gifts for children to give to grandparents

- a holiday calendar with photos of grandchildren
- a homemade card created for the grandparents
- blank video tapes or movies on tape
- toy gifts and games that grandparents can enjoy and play with children (especially when grandparents visit the homes of their grandchildren, or vise versa)
- give grandparents a tree ornament with the baby's picture on it as each grandchild joins the family
- arrange for each grandchild to send one tulip bulb for their grandparents' garden
- slippers
- a throw blanket

- a jogging suit
- a family tree picture Glue on family pictures, or have the children draw a likeness of family members. Show multiple generations— grandparents on the tree trunk, children as branches, grandchildren in outer foliage.
- a family photo frame (with each subsequent Christmas, present grandparents with an updated photograph)

Special commemoratives

The President of the United States will sign cards for people celebrating their eightieth birthday or older, and for couples celebrating their fiftieth wedding anniversary or more. Send requests, at least six weeks in advance, to: Attention: Greeting Office, The White House, Office of Communications, Washington, D.C. 20500. Include the birthdate or anniversary date, complete name (including Mr., Mrs., or Ms.), street address, city, state, and ZIP code of the person(s) to whom you want the greeting sent. If you want the greeting sent directly to you, include your address.

People confined to hospitals or convalescent homes, or who have health issues

- hand or body lotion, bath powder, luxurious soaps, warm/fuzzy socks or slippers
- lap robes or bed jackets
- family photographs, including pets (make b&w or color copies at a quick-copy store)
- a gift of coins to the patient who has access to gift shops, vending machines, pay phones, and newspaper/magazine stands.
- deck of playing cards (with large numbers)
- reading material or word puzzles (with pencil and eraser)

Visiting tips: Consider staying only 15 or 20 minutes in a hospital to avoid tiring patients. Don't sit on their bed; jiggling the bed can cause pain, especially to a surgical patient. It's probably best for everyone if you don't take children with you on a hospital visit. (Consider the potential emotional upset, or contagious nature of childhood illnesses.)

Chapter 12

Gift wrapping

The theory behind gift wrapping is to make gifts special. People display *wrapped* gifts, but rarely put unwrapped gifts on display. People seem to enjoy the creativity of the gift-wrapping process: according to the International Council of Shopping Centers, consumers spend nearly a third of their holiday cash in card and gift stores. Besides, wrapping gifts in unexpected ways adds to the holiday fun.

Considerations

• Decide early in the year whether you'll wrap your presents all at once, or as you purchase them.
• Plan to save the ribbons, bows and boxes that your gifts arrive in and use them next year— a great recycling idea and time-saver!
• Throughout the year, keep on hand a selection of solid red, green and white wrapping paper, and every occasion will be covered for the entire year. Vary ribbon color according to theme (birthday, anniversary, etc.)
• For another 'always ready' approach, keep on hand white butcher paper and rubber stamps.
• Encourage children to help wrap gifts. This may not only save you time, but it helps children feel capable and needed— a wonderful experience for everyone.

Wraps, bags, boxes, ribbons and gift tags
Wraps
• Wrap giant-size gifts in a paper Christmas tablecloth. It's less expensive and easier to work with than several sheets of wrapping paper. A flat bed sheet can also be used.
• Use old maps, calendars, photos from magazines, as a substitute for holiday wrap.
• Wrap food gifts in clear cellophane (available at florist supply or crafts stores) and tie with a length of luxurious ribbon.
• Consider using only red, green or cream paper; tie with a red ribbon or gold cord.

Natural wraps

- Brown or white paper with green holly
- Plain paper with raffia and a sprig of fir tree

Quick-wraps

- For a really fast wrap (with recycling benefits), save large plastic bags from small shops, etc. Turn the bags inside-out and put a gift inside (perhaps swathed with tissue). Twist the top of the bag, tie with a holiday-themed or colored bow, then trim any excess bag at the top, if desired. Pull at the top corners for a dramatic, flared appearance. Tape a gift card near the twisted part of the bag.
- Drop photos or small items into holiday-themed Ziplock sandwich bags. Purchase the colorful baggies at the grocers. For more information, call 1-800-428-4795.
- Cut a holiday message out of type from newspapers or magazines and glue to the front of a plain package. Create holiday graphics or festive type on your computer. Trim and paste to packages.
- For sturdy and unique wraps, buy remnant wallpaper. (You can buy last year's sample books at decorating stores.)
- For a car or travel-related gift, wrap it in an old (or new) map.
- Don't forget that many non-profit organizations sell gift wrap, as well as holiday cards.
- Wrap gifts using the Sunday comic section, foreign newspapers, or fashion pages.
- Use inexpensive, plastic holiday tablecloths or paper napkins as wrapping material.

Bags

- Wrap a large gift in a white trash bag and tie with ribbon. For a festive touch, add holiday stickers or self-sticking gold stars.
- Wrap a medium-sized gift in a fresh, new pillowcase; fold it back and pin it closed. White pillowcases with big red bows are especially festive.
- Fill lunch bags with treats and fold the top down. Punch two holes across the top and insert a candy cane through both holes.

Gift bags

- Have a selection of gift bags ready for any 'rush-wrapping' or odd-sized gifts.
- Don't forget that festive beverage bags (made of paper or cloth) are also good for wrapping long, slim items such as candles or long-handled kitchen utensils.

Boxes

- Pre-printed holiday boxes can really save your day *and back!* Plus, people tend to view the box as a gift in itself, and it can by recycled for other uses or next year's gift box. Pre-printed boxes are available at gift and stationery stores, import stores, and from catalogs.
- For the really industrious, get out your gold spraypaint and transform shoe boxes, cardboard tubes, or paper bags into special gift containers; finish them with a bright ribbon.

Packing tissue

- Wrap gifts in tissue and tie with ribbon (See 'Quick wraps' on previous page.)

Ribbons and such

- Buy large quantities of red, green, silver or gold metallic cord to tie down those loose ends.
- Twine, yarn and metallic string are fun to use, too. Tie on little berries or pine cones, etc., for a unique and virtually uncrushable (if they're plastic) finishing touch.
- Tie on cinnamon sticks or pine tree branches to add natural fragrance, as well as natural good looks.
- Tie items or packages with raffia ribbon; it's available at craft stores or from catalogs.
- Cut see-through material (such as chiffon) into long lengths (about 1-4 inches wide) and use as a lavish ribbon.
- Luxurious-to-simple ribbons are available through catalogs, as well as gift stores and almost everywhere else prior to the holidays.
- Consider dramatic gold or silver— nothing says 'magic' like metallic. Tie with wide velvet, satin or plaid ribbon.
- Strings of stars, snow flakes or reindeer on wire make a wonderful (and easy) decorative twist-and-tie ribbon (available at craft stores and from catalogs).
- Tie a small trinket to the bow (such as a small ornament, rattle, pet toy, or candy).

Gift tags

- Save old birthday and holiday cards to cut into small squares, fold in half, and use as gift tags. Backs of silver and gold cards are great for almost any gift throughout the year. You'll be recycling, too.
- Use rubber stamps and decorative-border scissors to brighten cards and gift-wrap. (These items are available from craft and greeting card stores, as well as catalogs.)

New packaging approaches

- Self-seal bags for wrapping CDs, audio cassettes and video tapes are usually available where you make your entertainment purchase.

One-stop shopping

- For a consolidated effort when shopping for gift wrap and accessories, don't forget your local stationery store. You may also find some interesting and useful gifts.
- Stop by a fabric store and purchase several yards of a light, inexpensive material (such as organza or Christmas-print cotton fabric) to use as a unique and easy-to-work-with wrapping medium.) This is an especially helpful tip for those hard-to-wrap gifts. You can also find collections of unique ribbons, tassels, and braids to finish wrapped gifts.
- Florists' supply stores are a great resource for many unique touches and ribbon, as well as large sheets of white or see-through paper.
- Crafts stores are terrific for all kinds of novel items.

Chapter 13

Holiday cards

Time-saving strategies
* Use self-adhesive stamps and return labels on envelopes
* Have a rubber stamp made with your name and address to use year 'round
* Create a database (computer list) of your holiday addresses. Print the addresses onto adhesive address labels (or pay a young relative or to do this for you on their computer). You can add a design element, or use festive pre-printed address labels (with an empty space for the address).
* *Really* save time by sending holiday postcards. You'll avoid the effort of stuffing envelopes, and save money on postage and cards.
* Order holiday cards from a non-profit organization or charity. Your purchase contributes to a good cause and saves shopping time.
* To save time and have fun, pick a night for the entire family to sign, address and decorate holiday cards.
* Late with your cards? Don't worry! Cards sent after Christmas can double as thank you or greeting cards for the New Year.

Sentiments
* It's always nice to add a charming, humorous or touching sentiment to the card before signing your name. However, personal notes are even better. (Don't forget to use larger print for older people.)

Mailing
* Our friends at the post office (Step away from the gun!) tell us that domestic holiday letters, cards, and packages should be mailed by early December (of *this* year). More time is necessary for international mail.

Storage/Recycling
* Recycle cards by cutting the front page from the back— instant holiday postcards for next year!

- Send your castoff cards to St. Jude's Ranch for Children, 100 St. Jude's St., Boulder City, NV 89005, a non-profit organization that cuts and pastes the artwork on recycled paper stock and then resells the cards.
- Used holiday cards can be reworked and help fund cystic fibrosis research. Send to: Cystic Fibrosis Research, c/o Myrtie Boor, 98 Via Cimarron, Monterey, CA 93940

Advanced Storage

- Keep all the family photographs (received in holiday cards) in a separate photo album; allow several pages for each family. You'll love seeing the changes as the years pass. Don't forget to list everyone's name on the back of the photos— it will help you remember names of new spouses, children and new members of the family.

Chapter 14
Holiday decorating, tips, and tools
Christmas trees (also known as 'The Fir Trade')
Cut trees

- Remember to put protective material under the tree's container to protect floors and carpets from water.
- Find a local cut-your-own tree farm by calling the National Christmas Tree Association at (414) 276-6410.
- Have a perfect tree delivered right to your door by calling Toll-Free Trees. Order a magnificent seven-foot Douglas Fir or 24-inch hand-decorated wreaths by dialing 1-800-540-3391. Prices at press time were: trees, $59.00; wreaths, $24.00 Makes a good gift idea, too.

Living trees

- Keep the soil of a live tree moist (while preventing spills) by placing several ice cubes on the soil each day.

Alternative choices

- Display a large wreath instead of a tree
- Decorate a large indoor plant
- If you're always traveling or visiting distant relatives for the holidays, why not skip the tree at your home this year?

Boughs

- Purchase cut boughs at a florist or tree stand. (First, ask if the boughs are being given away vs. being sold.) Use them to add visual, as well as olfactory, delight without the two-week Christmas tree watering vigil.
- Line the center of your holiday table with boughs. Metallic stars, etc., on wire can be tucked into the boughs for an impressive touch (and can be reused in following years in various applications— for topping gifts, decorating trees or other plants.)

Table and serving embellishments
- Inexpensive Christmas-print cotton fabric can be used as a beautiful covering for an extended dining room table or to dress up a folding table. Purchase your selection at a fabric store.
- Dramatically dress up your holiday buffet by adding tied bunches of parsley, or other fresh herbs, behind or beneath a serving dish. You may also stick long chives into bare spots as aromatic accents. You can even use the herbs in stews, etc., after their 'star quality' has been admired.
- Nestle serving dishes in baskets for a warm, rustic ambiance.

Room decorations
- String up tiny, white lights in various rooms for a dramatic and memorable touch. (You get extra points for placing the lights so that they will reflect in wall-mounted mirrors.)
- Appeal to all the senses during the holidays. Think of decorations in terms of sound, sight, smell and touch. Add spices such as cinnamon and nutmeg to a small pot of simmering water. Switch on your oven fan to waft the scents outdoors for your guests to enjoy as they approach your home.

Suggested mood music
Nat 'King' Cole, *Christmas Song* (Capitol/EMI Records)
Emmylou Harris, *Light of the Stable* (Warner Bros. Records)
Aaron Neville's *Soulful Christmas* (A&M Records)
Johnny Mathis, *Merry Christmas* (Columbia)
Willie Nelson, *Pretty Paper* (Columbia Records)
Wynton Marsalis, *Crescent City Christmas Card* (Columbia Records)
Elvis Presley, *Elvis' Christmas Album* (RCA Records)
Barbra Streisand, *A Christmas Album* (Columbia Records)
Darlene Love, The Ronettes, The Crystals, Bob B. Soxx & Blue Jeans, *A Christmas Gift For You from Phil Spector* (Phil Spector Records)
John Fahey, *John Fahey Chistmas Guitar* (Rounder Records)
Placido Domingo, Diana Ross, Jose Carreras, *Christmas in Vienna* (Sony Classical)
Various artists, *Acoustic Christmas* (CBS Records)

Availability
You can purchase or order these albums and CDs from your favorite music store, or on-line from http://cdnow.com; or www.musicblvd.com

Chapter 15
Holiday Food, Beverages and Quick Recipes

Loosen your belts: the holidays are baaaaack!
Your goal: to avoid exhaustion.

Holiday food and beverage strategy

Intersperse purchased and prepared foods with homemade foods. The same theory goes for plants: mix real and fake plants to fool the eye. It works! Use catalogs and their incredible selection of delicious prepared foods.

At home with guests

- To save time (and build confidence), build your buffet around a purchased Honey-Baked ham, smoked turkey, or other prepared entree. Add fragrant rolls and pots of gourmet mustards to create a wonderful buffet following the main meal, or use this idea for your holiday dinner by adding several side dishes, breads and festive beverages. An extra side dish or two will help you cope with last-minute guests.

- Enjoy a special dinner feast on Christmas Eve (with generous amounts of planned-for leftovers). On Christmas Day, you can kick back and enjoy being with one another rather than spending all day in the kitchen. Serve pastries for an informal brunch while you open gifts, make spur-of-the-moment sandwiches during the day, and have Christmas Eve leftovers for a casual supper.

- On December 24th, hit all of your favorite food stores— the bakery, fish market, gourmet food shop, chocolate shop— and buy only prepared food. You'll be able to nibble through Christmas Eve and Christmas Day. It's a real treat of wonderful food and you don't have to cook.

On your own

- Order a 'Special Dinner for One', to be delivered to your door or to someone who would really appreciate this gesture. The price is $55, plus $14.95 for shipping. The total number of orders is limited to 4,000, so order early! Call Food from Home at: 1-800-235-7070.

- Really escape the kitchen by ordering a holiday party for twelve from Food from Home at 1-800-235-7070. Prices (at print time) start at $150, plus $20 for shipping. The total number of orders is limited to 4,000. A special note: If you order early, you'll receive everything you need for your table. (In a show of understanding for their consumer's mind-set, the table items are disposable.)

Beverages

Offer refreshing, tangy and colorful beverages to your guests. A cranberry/sorbet beverage in a pretty prechilled bowl combines the best of both worlds. Order wine directly from wineries or catalogs to have them shipped to your door.

Food that's fast

Time out for a brief announcement. Speaking of *fast* recipes, check out *The 2-Ingredient Cookbook*, at your local library or bookstore. The cookbook makes a great holiday gift (suitable for all ages, and it's easy to wrap and mail). Brought to you by the fine folks at Meridian Publishing, Inc., who also published *Christmas Shortcuts*. For more information, call 1-800-270-2116.

Optional holiday dining facilities

You may decide to have a wonderful holiday off-site (or pamper someone special), but you must plan *far* ahead to ensure reservations (confirmed in writing). Many resorts, hotels, cruise ships, and bed-and-breakfasts offer special carefree holiday packages. This idea is terrific for people who are not welded to the more traditional holiday festivities, or for people who do not enjoy holiday family gatherings, need a change of pace, or enjoy meeting new people.

Chapter 16
Entertainment/Learning/Sharing

• There are many ways to celebrate the holidays in addition to Christmas, Hanukkah and, in many African-American communities, Kwanzaa. Customs vary according to personal, cultural, and religious beliefs, as well as geographical location. You may want to include a new food or recipe in your dinner feast, possibly adding something from another country's traditional holiday celebration. Learning about other cultures is important and these shared experiences can be delicious!

• Include nature in your holiday celebration. Teach children to respect nature's creatures by decorating an outdoor tree or plant with edible treats for birds, such as strings of popcorn. Set out seed, or put suet inside a net produce bag and hang it from a rain gutter near a window, and enjoy watching birds as they consume their holiday treat.

• Once you've decided what to eliminate from the holiday rat race, include an activity to give the day more meaning. Remember to enjoy the simple pleasures of ice skating, walking with a group, and reaching beyond your familiar circle to do something for others.

• Line up baby sitters for social outings now, *before* scheduling them becomes impossible.

• Don't be afraid to do something non-traditional. Think barbecue or camping, etc.

• Loneliness can be lessened by getting involved in a service project with others. Donate food, gifts, or dinners to needy families.

• To get into the holiday spirit, you might consider visiting hospitals, volunteering for a children's reading at your local library, or availing your services at a local charitable event.

• Events for children are often held at local libraries

• Consider family-friendly events/traditions such as outdoor games or Christmas fairs, etc.

- During the holiday gatherings, telephone family and/or friends who live too far away to attend. This helps to mitigate people's feelings of loneliness or isolation.

- Ask the oldest person at your holiday table, or special guest, to light the candles or offer a toast. This is a terrific way to pay tribute to guests and older relatives.

- Add to your gift list at least one coupon to do something with, or for, someone. Encourage children to add this item to their 'holiday-giving list'. It will help to teach them about the gift of spending time with people. This may be your most appreciated and precious gift of all.

- Ask everyone at your special gatherings to sign a card addressed to someone who could not attend the festivities this year. After dinner, take a walk (if that's still physically possible) to a mailbox and send the message on its way.

- Purchase from a catalog or music store, or borrow from the local library, special holiday tapes, videos or CDs. Young children (as well as adults) enjoy listening to an audio tape of a Christmas story or holiday songs after dinner. The holiday songs can provide a delightful audio background to enrich your holiday gathering.

Community

- You may want to attend religious services as a family. Spirituality, customs and traditions are an integral part of the holidays for many people. Many churches hold special events and ceremonies during the holidays.
- Consider hospital or retirement home visits to friends or family members. Make an audio (or video) tape of various friends or family members sending cheery holiday greetings or special messages. (Be sure to check ahead at the facility for the type of playback equipment available.)
- Attend local charity (entertainment) events.
- Sing carols in your neighborhood.
- Most neighborhoods have certain areas where people in the community go all out when decorating the exteriors of their homes. Drive there and walk down the sidewalks to experience a 'small village' kind of holiday feeling. This may be a good place to take your 'road show' of carolers.
- Do something for the world around you. Donate a small amount of money or time to the charity that interests you. Plant a tree. It's then that the holiday spirit will warm you.

Chapter 17

Holiday survival tips

- Celebrate the holidays by taking care of yourself. Be aware when you feel tired, overextended, angry, tense or depressed.

- Get clear about your priorities. Ask yourself if the event is 'fun' or 'duty'?

- Drain your tensions in a healthy way. Get some fresh air, walk, exercise, call a friend.

- Accept feelings of sadness, anger or frustration— these are normal.

- Accept that some people may not celebrate the holidays every year. They may take a year off and opt for a family ski trip instead. Some people simply may not be up to the emotional challenge of the holiday season. By accepting these differences in people, you set a good example for your children.

- Understand that you can't do it all. Don't rush to accomplish the impossible. Do what absolutely needs to be done and let go of the rest.

- Make time to enjoy your friends and family. Pause to enjoy this special time of year.

Chapter 18

Different holiday approaches

- Consider holding back-to-back parties. The decorations will be up and your residence clean (or fairly so) on two consecutive days/nights. You can purchase or prepare food for both occasions, as well as having all your serving pieces at hand.

- Take advantage of Internet holiday shopping tips and time-savers.

- Have your children cruise holiday web sites for games and fun, such as Yahoo/Yahooligans (for kids)

- Search for unique gifts (check the Internet, as well as catalogs,museums and import stores)

- Shop for Christmas gifts while on vacation; mail them to your home address.

- Compile a list of quick (already wrapped) gifts and the stores that carry them.

- Purchase quick (already wrapped) food gifts in bulk (fruit, nuts, treats, etc.)

- Remember to scan speciality stores, such as: toy stores, book stores, stationery stores, museum shops, gourmet food shops, beauty-supply or health-food stores (natural soaps and cosmetics) for unusual gift ideas for young and old.

Chapter 19
Lists of catalogs

•**The Great Directory of Undiscovered Catalogs**, (407) 989-5346; Publisher Inquiry Services, 951 Broken Sound Parkway NW, Building 190, P.O. Box 5057, Boca Raton, FL 33431

•**The Original Catalog of Canadian Catalogs**, by Elie and Leila Albala, (514) 658-6205; lists over 1,000 catalogs, $16.95 US postpaid (price at time of publication);

•Alpe Publishing, PO Box 203, Chalbly, Quebec, Canada J3L 4B3 Fax: (514) 658-3514

Children's gift catalogs

•**Animal Town,** *toys, games and books for cooperative learning and endless fun,* P.O. Box 485, Healdsburg, CA 95448

•**Dover Christmas Book Catalog,** *over 1,200 beautiful books, cards and stickers*; 31 East 2nd St., Mineola, NY 11501 (Note: No telephone or credit card orders accepted.)

•**Kids & things,** *children's educational books, games, toys, videos and software,* 1-800-243-0464; P.O. Box 14607, Madison, WI 53714

•**Learn & Play**, *imaginative, fun and creative gifts,* 1-800-247-6106; 45 Curiosity Lane, P.O. Box 1822, Peoria, Illinois 61656

•**Young Explorers**, *creative educational products,* 1-800-239-7577; 825 S.W. Frontage Road, Ft. Collins, CO 80522

Gourmet and Speciality Foods

•**De Brito Chocolate Factory,** *chocolate-covered fruit,* 1-800-588-3886; 160-Briggs Rd., Hollister, CA 95023

•**Devine Delights,** *a taste of heaven,* 1-800-443-2836; 24 Digital Drive, Suite 10, Novato, CA 94949

•**Ethel M Chocolates**, 1-800-438-4356; P.O. Box 98505, Las Vegas, NV 89193; www.ethelm.com

•**Fancy Foods Gourmet Club,** *award-winning gourmet food,* 1-800-576-3548; 300-E N. Stonestreet Ave., Rockville, MD 20850

•**Frontier Soups,** *special gift baskets of soups and bread,* 1-800-253-0550; 970 North Shore Drive, Lake Bluff, IL 60044

•**Mauna Loa,** *food products from Hawaii,* 1-800-832-9993; 6523 N. Galena Road, P.O. Box 1772, Peoria, IL 61656

- **Missouri Dandy Pantry,** *savory holiday baked goods,*
  1-800-872-6879;   414 North St., Stockton, MO 65785
- **Norm Thompson**, *food and floral gifts,* 1-800-547-1160;
  P.O. Box 3999, Portland, OR 97208
- **Pinnacle Orchards,** *food baskets and tins,* 1-800-759-1232;
  P.O. Box 616, Maumee, OH 43537
- **Rent Mother Nature**, *fruit and nut tree leases + delivery to your door,*
  1-800-232-4048 or (617) 354-5430; 52 New Street, P.O. Box 38013,
  Cambridge, Massachusetts 02238
- **SeaBear**, *smoked salmon products from Washington,* 1-800-645-3474;
  605 30th St., P.O. Box 591, Anacortes, WA 98221;
  www.amsquare.com/seabear/
- **See's Candies**, *holiday-themed and regular high-quality chocolates,*
  1-800-347-7337; P.O. Box 'S', Culver City, CA 90231

Health and Lifestyle Gifts

- **BackSaver,** *gifts of health and comfort,* 1-800-251-2225;
  53 Jeffrey Avenue, Holliston, MA 01746
- **SelfCare**, *health and comfort gifts,* 1-800-345-3371; 5850 Shellmound St.,
  Emeryville, CA 94608; e-mail: SlfCare@aol.com
- **Travel 2000**, *travel gear items,* 1-800-903-8728; P.O. Box 27156,
  Lansing, MI 48909

Holiday Decorations and Gifts

- **Bakers and Builders,** *gingerbread houses, $23-30,* (207) 236-4871;
  4851 Melvin Heights Road, Camden, ME 04843 (Send a SASE
  to receive a free catalog.)
- **Ballard Designs**, *accents for the home and garden,* 1-800-367-2775;
  1670 DeFoor Ave. NW, Atlanta, GA 30318; www.ballard-designs.com
- *Brainstorms, wacky toys, brainy inventions, creative inspirations and
  madcap gifts,* 1-800-231-6000; 8221 Kimball, Skokie, IL   60076
- **Bright Ideas**, *personalized Christmas tree ornaments, $15-30,*
  (201) 343-4150; 101 Riverside Square Mall, Hackensack, NJ 07601
- **Brookstone,** *hard-to-find-tools and gifts,* 1-800-926-7000;
  17 Riverside St., Nashua, New Hampshire 03062
- **Casual Living**, *distinctive gifts and holiday items,* 1-800-843-1881;
  P.O. Box 31273, Tampa, FL 33631
- **Caswell-Massey**, *bath and body gift productions,* 1-800-326-0500;
  100 Enterprise Place, Dover, Delaware 19904

- **Coldwater Creek,** *a north county catalog,* 1-800-262-0040; One Coldwater Creek Drive, Sandpoint, Idaho 83864
- **Colonial Garden Kitchens,** *kitchen gifts and gadgets,* 1-800-245-3399; P.O. Box 66, Hanover, PA 17333
- **Company Store,** *linens, luxurious throws, and clothing,* 1-800-285-3696; 500 Company Store Rd., La Crosse, Wisconsin 54601
- **Crate & Barrel,** 1-800-323-5461
- **Current,** *correspondence supplies and tools, as well as gifts and stickers,* 1-800-525-7170; The Current Building, Colorado Springs, CO 80941
- **David Kay,** *garden and home,* 1-800-535-9917; P.O. Box 2050, Omaha, Nebraska 68103
- **Duncraft,** *specialities for birdfeeding,* 1-800-593-5656; Penacook, NH 033303
- **Edmund Scientific's,** *catalog for educators, students and inventors,* (609) 547-8880; 101 East Gloucester Pike, Barrington, NJ 08007
- **Embossing Arts Co.,** *rubber art stamps and cardmaking supplies,* (541) 928-9898; P.O. Box 439, Tangent, OR 97389
- **Faith Mountain Company,** *gifts and clothing,* 1-800-822-7238; P.O. Box 199, Sperryville, VA 22740; www.FaithMountain.com
- **Front Gate,** *holiday items and furnishings,* 1-800-626-6488; 2800 Henkle Drive, Lebanon, OH 45036
- **Gardeners Eden,** *wreaths, gifts and plants,* 1-800-822-9600; P.O. Box 7307, San Francisco, CA 94120-7307
- **Gardener's Supply Company,** *garden tools & holiday food gifts,* 1-800-955-3370; 128 Intervale Rd., Burlington, VT 05401
- **Gifts for Grandkids,** *a mix of traditional and modern toys to software,* 1-800-333-1707; c/o Genesis Direct, One Bridge Plaza, Suite 680, Fort Lee, NJ 07024
- **Herrington,** *gifts for enthusiasts of golf, travel, photography, fitness, and top-notch audio/video equipment,* 1-800-903-2878; 3 Symmes Dr., Londonderry, NH 03053
- **Hold everything,** *a contemporary collection of gifts that bring beauty to practicality,* 1-800-421-2264; P.O. Box 7807, San Francisco, CA 94120
- **Home Decorators Collection,** *furniture, lamps and gift items,* 1-800-245-2217; 2025 Concourse Drive, St. Louis, MO 63146
- **Horchow Collection,** *luxurious eclectic items,* 1-800-395-5397; P.O. Box 620048, Dallas, TX, 75262
- **Initials,** *distinctive personalized gifts,* 1-800-586-1600; 530 Execu tive Drive, Willowbrook, IL 60521
- **In the Company of Dogs,** *gifts and gear for dogs,* 1-800-924-5050; P.O. Box 7071, Dover, DE 19903

•**Into the Wind**, *kites, flags, windsocks and flying toys,*
1-800-541-0314; 1408 Pearl Street, Boulder, CO 80302
•**Jackson & Perkins**, *trees, wreaths, plants, and gifts,* 1-800-292-4769;
P.O. Box 1028, Medford, OR 97501
•**Joan Cook**, *housewares, home furnishings, gifts, and accessories,*
1-800-935-0971; 119 Foster Street, Peabody, MA 01960
•**Kitchen & Home**, *upscale household gifts,* 1-800-414-5544;
P.O. Box 72, Hanover, PA 17333
•**Levenger**, *gifts and tools for readers, paperweights for lawyers,*
1-800-544-0880; 420 S. Congress Ave., Delray Beach, Florida 33445
•**Lillian Vernon**, *inexpensive gifts and free personalization,*
1-800-285-5555; Virginia Beach, VA 23479
•**Mind's Eye**, *a century of holiday gifts,* 1-800-949-3333;
P.O. Box 6547, Chelmsford, Massachusetts 01824
•**MindWare**, *puzzles and games for curious minds,* 1-800-999-0398;
2720 Patton Road, Roseville, MN 55115
•**National Wildlife Federation**, *nature gifts,* 1-800-477-5560;
310 Tyson Drive, Winchester, VA 22603
•**Nature Company**, *gifts from and about nature,* 1-800-227-1114
•**Oriental Trading Co.**, *small, unique holiday-themed gifts and decora-*
tions, 1-800-228-2269; P.O. Box 2308, Omaha, NE 68103
•**Orvis,** *clothing and gifts,* 1-800-541-3541; Historic Route 7A,
Manchester, VT 05254
•**Paper Direct**, *'artsy' paper/stationery for computer printers,*
1-800-272-7377; 100 Plaza Drive, Secaucus, NJ 07094
•**Paragon**, *holiday and decorative items,* 1-800-343-3095 or
(401) 596-0134; 89 Tom Harvey Rd., Westerly, Rhode Island 02891
•**Past Times**, *gifts inspired by Great Britain's past,* 1-800-621-6020;
280 Summer St., Boston, MA 02210
•**Potpourri**, *collection of gifts & decorations,* 1-800-388-7798;
120 North Meadows Road, Medfield, MA 02052
•**Pottery Barn,** *fine household items and furniture,* 1-800-922-5507;
P.O. Box 7044, San Francisco, CA 94121
•**Recorded Books**, 1-800-638-1304
•**Seasons**, *gifts from books to jewelry,* 1-800-776-9677; P.O. Box 64545,
St. Paul, MN 55164
•**SelfCare**, *products and gifts for healthy living,* 1-800-345-3371;
5850 Shellmound St., Emeryville, CA 94608; e-mail: SlfCare@aol.com
•**Seventh Generation**, *gifts and products for a healthy planet,* Gaiam,
Inc., One Mill St., Suite A26, Burlington, VT 05401

- **Sharper Image**, *contemporary gifts and gadgets*, 1-800-344-4444;
  650 Davis Street, San Francisco, CA 94111
- **Signals,** *videos, checkbook covers and sweatshirts;* 1-800-570-1004;
  P.O. Box 64428, St. Paul, Minn 55164
- **Solutions**, *sensible gifts,* 1-800-342-9988; P.O. Box 6878,
  Portland, OR 97228
- **Stress Less,** *stress-relief products,* 1-800-555-3783; P.O. Box 52164,
  Atlanta, GA 30355
- **Sur La Table,** *gifts and fine equipment for domestic and professional
  kitchens,* 1-800-243-0852; 401 Terry Ave., North, Seattle, WA 98109
- **Terry's Village**, *festive decorations and heartwarming gifts,*
  1-800-200-4400; P.O. Box 2309, Omaha, NE 68103
- **Times Limited,** 1-800-366-4071
- **Treasure Chest,** *'seafaring gifts from the oceans of the world',*
  1-800-480-1258; 50 Misty Meadow Dr., Boynton Beach, FL 33462
- **Williams-Sonoma**, *gifts and equipment for cooks, as well as holiday
  food gifts*; 1-800-541-2233; P.O. Box 7456, San Francisco, CA 94120
- **Wireless,** *from neckties to puzzles, and other unusual items;*
  1-800-570-5003; P.O. Box 64422, St. Paul, Minn 55164

Holiday gift catalogs from non-profit organizations

- **Humane Society of the United States**, *children's books, holiday cards
  and calendars,* 1-800-486-2630; One Humane Way, Ridgely, MD 21685
- **Unicef** (United Nations Children's Fund), *cards and gifts,* 1-800-553-1200;
  Box 182233, Chattanooga, TN 37422

Museum catalogs
(unique gift ideas and holiday cards)

- **Art Institute of Chicago,** *museum shop catalog,*
  1-800-621-9337; Michigan Avenue at Adams St., Chicago, IL 60603
- **Metropolitan Museum of Art,** 1-800-468-7386;
  255 Gracie Station, New York, NY 10028

•**Museum of Fine Arts, Boston,** *scarves and jewelry,* 1-800-225-5592; P.O. Box 244, Avon, Mass. 02322-0244

•**Museum of Jewelry,** *period jewelry,* 1-800-835-2700; 3000 Larkin St., San Francisco, CA 94109

•**Museum of Modern Art, New York,** *napkin rings to furniture,* 1-800-447-6662; P.O. Box 2534, Westchester, PA 19380. A $2 donation is requested.

•**Smithsonian,** 1-800-322-0344; 7955 Angus Court, Springfield, VA 22153

Chapter 20
Post-holiday tips or... after all the tinsel has been swept away

- If you didn't have time to send holiday cards *before* the holidays, send them afterwards. People will still love hearing from you, and you'll probably have post-holiday news to share.

- Store your holiday trimmings in plastic snap-shut containers. Don't forget to label them to save you *lots* of excavation time in the future! Tupperware or Rubbermaid containers offer special containers (including wreath and ornament boxes) in which to protect delicate items from being crushed or damaged.

- Shop for holiday gifts while you're on vacation. Most people enjoy receiving regional gifts such as New Orleans pralines, Alaskan smoked salmon, or chocolate from Paris.

- Purchase holiday supplies, such as stamps and baking ingredients, weeks/ months in advance to avoid holiday lines and the supply/demand surge.

- Throughout the year, tuck away suitable gifts that you find on sale.

- Take advantage of post-holiday sales and buy wrapping paper, cards, ornaments and ribbons at discounted prices. (You might want to wait a few days after Christmas until the post-holiday shopping frenzy is over before you attempt this.)

- Make notes of what (gifts, events, food) went over especially well this past holiday.

- Write a note to yourself about whatever made you unhappy in December. Reread the note next spring or summer, when you will be ready to develop strategies to change things before next Christmas. If the thing you need to change is a family tradition, begin talking to your significant others or family members now. It will take six months for them to accept a new plan that takes your needs— not just theirs— into account.

Index

Notes